Multi-story SATs Fiction prep from CGP!

This Foundation SAT Buster is perfect for pupils who find KS2 English tough going. It's packed with friendly practice to steadily build up the Fiction Reading skills they'll need for the SATs in Year 6.

We've included plenty of helpful hints and tips along the way, plus example answers to show them what they're aiming for.

There are also fun self-assessment boxes for each topic, plus a scoresheet to keep track of their overall marks. We've thought of everything!

What CGP is all about

Our sole aim here at CGP is to produce the highest quality books — carefully written, immaculately presented and dangerously close to being funny.

Then we work our socks off to get them out to you — at the cheapest possible prices.

Contents

Section 1 – The Ghost

The Ghost 2
Fact Retrieval Questions 6
Inference Questions 8
Word Meaning Questions 10
Summary and Structure Questions 11

Section 2 – Visiting Day

Visiting Day 12
Fact Retrieval Questions 16
Inference Questions 18
Word Meaning Questions 20
Summary and Comparison Questions 21

Section 3 – Crocodile Tale

Crocodile Tale 22
Fact Retrieval Questions 26
Inference Questions 28
Word Meaning Questions 30
Summary and Prediction Questions 31

Section 4 – Ready for Take-Off

Ready for Take-Off 32
Fact Retrieval Questions 36
Inference Questions 38
Word Meaning Questions 40
Summary and Language Questions 41

Scoresheet 42

Published by CGP

Editors: Emily Forsberg, Melissa Gardner, Catherine Heygate, Katya Parkes, Rebecca Russell, Sean Walsh

ISBN: 978 1 78908 422 1

With thanks to Izzy Bowen and Juliette Green for the proofreading.
With thanks to Emily Smith for the copyright research.

Printed by Elanders Ltd, Newcastle upon Tyne.
Clipart from Corel®

Based on the classic CGP style created by Richard Parsons.

Here's what you have to do:

In Year 6 you have to take some tests called the SATs.
This book will help you do well in the reading bit of the tests.

The reading paper will test you on eight different reading elements:

2a Word Meanings   **2c** Summarising   **2e** Predictions   **2g** Language

2b Fact Retrieval   **2d** Inferences   **2f** Structure   **2h** Comparisons

These elements are used to see how well you can understand texts.

To help you improve your reading skills, this book has separate question pages for each of the reading elements — so you always know which one you are practising.

This is a Tellastaurius — it can read and understand even the trickiest fiction texts.

Your aim is to become a Tellastaurius.

Work through the questions in the book. When you finish a section, add up your marks and write them in the scoresheet at the end of the book.

Then, put a tick in the box at the end of the topic to show how you got on.

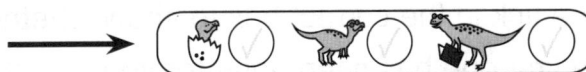

If you got a lot of questions wrong, put a tick in the circle on the left. Don't worry — every Tellastaurius has to start somewhere. Read the texts again carefully, then have another go.

If you're nearly there but you're still a bit wobbly on some questions, put a tick in the middle circle. Ask your teacher to help you work out the areas you need more practice on.

If you felt really confident and got nearly all the answers right, tick the circle on the right.

Congratulations — you're a Tellastaurius!

Fact Retrieval Questions

FACT RETRIEVAL questions are all about finding bits of information in the text.
Read 'The Ghost' again, then see how you get on with these questions about the story.

1)   Write down **one** thing the boys put on the floor when getting ready
     for their sleepover.

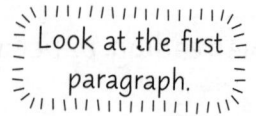

Look at the first paragraph.

....

_____
1 mark

2)   Find and copy **one** thing Mrs Amsel told the boys to do at the start of the story.

....

_____
1 mark

3)   Whose idea was it to tell ghost stories? Circle your answer.

| **Mrs Amsel's** | **Davit's** | **Nish's** | **Olly's** |

_____
1 mark

4)   Put a tick in the correct box to show whether each statement is true or false.
     The first one has been done for you.

	True	False
The boys thought it was too early to go to sleep.	✓	
Davit's mum told the boys a ghost story.		
Nish was holding a torch while he told his story.		

_____
1 mark

5)   Read the paragraph beginning **'"I do," said Nish...'**
     Give **one** type of treasure that is mentioned in this paragraph.

....

_____
1 mark

The Ghost

This story is about three boys who are at a sleepover.
Davit, Olly and Nish start telling each other scary ghost stories,
but then real life starts getting pretty scary too...

What to do

1) Turn over the page, and read the story **The Ghost**.

2) Then have another read through it. It'll help make sure you've really understood every part of the story.

3) Once you feel nice and familiar with what happens in the story, have a go at the questions.

Turn the page. ➤

"It's not," said Olly. "Ghosts aren't real, Davit."

"It is!" Davit insisted. "I went there yesterday and I saw a ghost with my own eyes!" He paused, then lowered his voice dramatically. "I crept across the long grass as quietly as I could and looked through a gap in the boards over the windows. It was really dark inside, but I saw something move."

Olly shook his head, but Nish was staring at Davit with wide eyes.

"Suddenly," Davit continued, "a gust of wind blew right through me. You remember how hot it was yesterday?"

"Boiling hot," Nish answered.

"Well, this wind was ice cold. I was shivering like a leaf. Then all the dogs in the neighbourhood started barking at once."

"Wow," breathed Nish.

"Then a big white shape appeared out of the darkness. It was like a person, but I couldn't see its face. It was coming right at me. I ran as fast as I could away from the house. I could hear it behind me, but I just kept running and running. It followed me all the way home."

Both boys were concentrating on Davit now, his face glowing with torchlight in the gloom of the living room. Suddenly, something white leapt from the shadows and sped across the floor, lunging at Olly.

Olly yelled and jumped to his feet. "Gh-ghost!" he cried.

Nish scrambled up too, looking around wildly. "Where did it go?"

Davit burst out laughing. He stood up and turned on the lights. "It's just Rex," he said, as a small, white creature jumped out from a pile of blankets, barking happily and wagging his tail. "I can't believe you were scared of him. That's enough ghost stories for one night!"

The Ghost

Davit's mum stood in the living room doorway. She waited patiently while the three boys covered the floor in pillows, blankets and duvets in preparation for their sleepover.

"Okay boys," she said. "Don't stay up too late, don't disturb the dog and make sure you brush your teeth before you go to sleep."

"We will, Mrs Amsel," Olly and Nish said together.

As his mum closed the door, Davit turned to his friends. "What do you want to do? I'm not tired at all."

"We can't go to sleep yet," said Olly. "It's so early."

"Let's tell ghost stories," said Nish.

Davit turned off the lights, throwing the room into darkness. He switched on a torch. "Does anyone know any good ones?"

"I do," said Nish. Davit handed him the torch, and Nish turned it upwards so the light glowed creepily over his face. "There once was this pirate who sailed the high seas and collected loads of treasure, like gold coins and jewels and stuff. After he died, he came back and haunted the treasure."

"What did he do to people if they found the treasure?" asked Davit.

"Don't know," said Nish, his forehead creasing. "I think he just sort of hovered nearby."

"Huh," Olly laughed. "So if someone stole a coin and put it in their pocket, what would happen? Would he just follow them round, keep them company while they did their shopping?"

"That's a rubbish story," said Davit. He took the torch from Nish. "My turn. Let me tell you a real ghost story. You know the old house on the way to school? The one with the cobwebs, the boarded-up windows and all those scary-looking trees outside? It's *haunted*."

Keep turning...

Fact Retrieval Questions

2b

6) Read the paragraph beginning '**"That's a rubbish story...'**
   According to Davit's story, where is the haunted house?

| next door to Davit's house | in the countryside | next to a busy road | on the way to school |

Circle your answer.

_____
1 mark

7) How does Davit describe the trees outside the haunted house?

| scary-looking | enormous | sturdy | twisted |

Circle your answer.

_____
1 mark

8) According to Nish, what was the weather like the day before?

....

_____
1 mark

9) Read the paragraph beginning '**"Then a big white shape appeared...'**
   What did the ghost in Davit's story do?

Tick **one** box.

It followed Davit home. ☐

It touched Davit on the shoulder. ☐

It asked Davit to leave. ☐

It invited Davit into the house. ☐

_____
1 mark

Tellastauriuses love to do triple somersault dives into pools of facts. How did you find this page? Tick a box.

Inference Questions

INFERENCE questions get you to think about the story more deeply. To answer the questions on these pages, you'll have to really think about what's happening in the story.

1) Where does the story take place?

Davit's house	**Olly's house**	**Nish's house**

Circle your answer.

_____
1 mark

2) Why do you think Davit turned off the lights when they started telling ghost stories?

Tick **one** box.

Because his mum told him to ☐

To make the ghost stories scarier ☐

So that they wouldn't disturb Rex ☐

Because he wanted to go to sleep ☐

_____
1 mark

3) Circle the word that best describes the pirate in Nish's story.

strong	**kind**	**rich**	**poor**

_____
1 mark

4) Read from '"**That's a rubbish story...**' to '**...saw something move.**"'
How can you tell that no one lives in the house? Give **one** way.

....

....

_____
1 mark

2d # Inference Questions

5) Read the paragraph beginning **"'Then a big white shape appeared...'**
What do you think Davit was thinking when he saw the ghost?

Tick **one** box.

He wanted to talk to the ghost. ☐

He thought the ghost was very ugly. ☐

He thought the ghost was funny. ☐

He wanted to get away from the ghost. ☐

1 mark

6) Read from **'Both boys were concentrating...'** to **'"Where did it go?"'**
Why were Nish and Olly scared?

| Davit's face looked scary. | There was a loud noise. | They thought they saw a ghost. | Davit's story got really scary. |

Circle your answer.

1 mark

7) Read the last paragraph of the text.
Find and copy a sentence which suggests that Davit wasn't scared.

....

1 mark

8) Who do you think Rex is?

Think about what Rex does and how he acts.

....

1 mark

A Tellastaurius eats inference questions for breakfast.
How did you get on? Tick one of the boxes.

2a **Word Meaning Questions**

WORD MEANING questions will test your vocabulary skills. Read the story again, then try the questions on this page to check you have understood the words in the text.

1) **'"I think he just sort of hovered nearby."'**
Circle the word which means the same as **'hovered'** in this sentence.

| chased | floated | hunted | whispered |

_____
1 mark

2) Read from **'"Well, this wind was ice cold..."'** to **'"Wow," breathed Nish.'**
Which word could be replaced by the word 'shaking'?

....

_____
1 mark

3) **'...glowing with torchlight in the gloom of the living room.'**
Circle the word that means the same as **'gloom'** in this sentence.

Think about which word would make sense in the sentence.

| darkness | cold | silence | light |

_____
1 mark

4) Read the paragraph beginning **'Both boys were concentrating...'**
Which of these is closest in meaning to **'leapt'**? Tick **one** box.

ran ☐   jumped ☐

crept ☐   shouted ☐

_____
1 mark

Tellastauriuses like nothing more than answering word meaning questions. How did you find them?

2c

Summary Questions

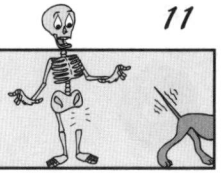

SUMMARY questions get you to think about big chunks of the story, or even the story as a whole. Read through 'The Ghost' again, then have a go at these questions.

1) Put these summaries of paragraphs in the order they happened in the story. The first one has been done for you.

The boys saw Rex. ☐

Davit told a ghost story. ☐

The boys decided what to do. **1**

Nish told a ghost story. ☐

_____
1 mark

2) Read from "'**That's a rubbish story...**' to '**...saw something move.**'"
   Which phrase best summarises these paragraphs? Circle your answer.

Turning the lights off in the room	**Saying goodnight to Davit's mum**	**Describing the haunted house**	**Something jumping out at Olly**

_____
1 mark

2f

Structure Question

STRUCTURE questions get you to think about all the parts that make up a story. Give this question a go to see how well you understand the different parts of the text.

1) Read the quotations below, then match each one to the part of the story it shows. One has been done for you.

'throwing the room into darkness'   setting

'Let me tell you a real ghost story.'   action

'Olly yelled and jumped to his feet.'   speech

_____
1 mark

A Tellastaurius is happiest when it's answering summary and structure questions. How did you do?

Fact Retrieval Questions

FACT RETRIEVAL questions are all about picking out information from the text. It's time to put your detective's hat on and start searching through the story for the answers.

1) Where is Tinashe's primary school?

Look carefully at the information you're given about the two schools.

| opposite Caynton High | down the road from Caynton High | in the next village to Caynton High |

Circle your answer.

1 mark

2) Who is Miss Ellis?

Tick **one** box.

The head teacher at Caynton High ☐

Tinashe's primary school teacher ☐

A teacher who is the Head of Year 7 ☐

A tour guide at Caynton High ☐

1 mark

3) What colour was Miss Ellis's blouse?

Look out for a colour word in the text near to Miss Ellis's name.

....

1 mark

4) Read the paragraph beginning **'As they walked...'**
Write down **one** thing that Miss Ellis explained about classes.

....

....

1 mark

Keep turning...

Visiting Day

The high school looked so strange to Tinashe as she followed her classmates along the driveway. Even though her primary school was just down the road, visiting day was the first time she had passed through those monstrous iron gates and trudged towards the towering brick buildings of Caynton High.

Tinashe gulped. She was dreading the move to high school in September. She liked her school and her lessons and her teacher, but at high school, all of that would change. She was deep in worried thought when a woman approached the group and asked them to follow her. She introduced herself as Miss Ellis, the Head of Year 7.

As the group climbed up and down staircases and snaked in and out of hallways that all looked the same, Tinashe fixed her eyes on Miss Ellis's bright yellow blouse and tried not to lose sight of it. How did people not get lost?

As they walked, Miss Ellis explained about classes and bells and timetables. She told the group that classes would be made up of pupils from lots of different primary schools, and that their classmates would be different for every subject. Tinashe sighed — making friends was another thing to worry about.

They went past more rooms. Computer rooms, music rooms, drama rooms, art rooms, a sports hall... It seemed like every subject had its own room and its own equipment.

"These are our science labs," said Miss Ellis. "Take a look. You probably won't have anything like this at your current school."

Everyone peered in through the windows for a closer look. Tinashe stood on her tiptoes, stretching her neck to see over her classmates.

For as long as she could remember, she had found science fascinating. She loved TV programmes about anything from outer space to the rainforest. Instead of toys, she had asked for a chemistry set and a microscope for Christmas, and her bedroom had shelves full of books about famous inventors.

Her eyes widened as she peeked into the lab. It looked exactly the same as pictures she'd seen in books. The room was full of strangely tall tables, and chairs with long, thin legs to match. The walls were covered with posters of things like the inside of the human body and the planets going around the Sun.

The students were in the middle of a lesson. They wore white coats over their uniforms and had glasses to protect their eyes — they looked just like proper scientists. Glass beakers filled with mysterious liquids were balanced over bright blue flames. The students were carefully adding strange, coloured powders to the glass jars a little bit at a time. Every so often, one of the jars would start bubbling or change colour when something new was added.

"It's almost magical!" she gasped. "It's like a potions class!" She desperately wanted to go inside, but Miss Ellis called the group to continue on their tour.

Tinashe watched a little longer. Yes, getting used to Caynton High would be difficult, but now she couldn't wait for September to arrive.

Visiting Day

'Visiting Day' is a story about a girl called Tinashe who goes to visit the high school she will be moving to next year. Tinashe is really nervous about moving schools, but that might be about to change...

What to do

1) Turn over the page, and read the story **Visiting Day**.

2) Then go back and have another read of the story.
   It's the best way to make sure you've understood it all.

3) After you've done that, it's time to start working through the questions.

Welcome to
Caynton
High

Turn the page. ➡

Fact Retrieval Questions

5) Put a tick in the correct box to show whether each statement is true or false.
   The first one has been done for you.

	True	False
Tinashe wasn't worried about making new friends.		✓
The group walked past a sports hall.		
Miss Ellis thought the children had labs at their primary school.		

1 mark

6) Read the paragraph beginning **'For as long as...'**
   What Christmas presents did Tinashe ask for? Tick **two** boxes.

   Make sure you read the paragraph really carefully.

   some science books ☐   a microscope ☐

   a chemistry set ☐   toys ☐

1 mark

7) Read the paragraph beginning **'The students were in the middle...'**
   Write down **one** item of clothing that the students were wearing.

   ....

1 mark

8) What were the students adding to the glass jars?

   ....

1 mark

Tellastauriuses love fact retrieval questions — they even practise them at the weekend. How did you get on?

Inference Questions

INFERENCE questions ask you to work things out from the text, so you'll need to think hard about what's happening in the story. Read 'Visiting Day' again, then try these questions.

1) Read the paragraph beginning **'The high school looked...'**
    Give **one** way Caynton High seems scary.

    Look at how the school is described.

    ....

    1 mark

2) Read the paragraph beginning **'As the group climbed...'**
    The inside of Caynton High seems

    Think about the language that the writer uses.

    | exciting | messy | confusing | boring |

    Circle your answer.

    1 mark

3) Why did Tinashe stare at Miss Ellis's blouse and try not to lose sight of it?

    Tick one box.

    She really liked the blouse. ☐

    She didn't want to get lost. ☐

    Her mum had the same blouse. ☐

    She was far away from Miss Ellis. ☐

    Think carefully about what is happening in the rest of the paragraph.

    1 mark

4) **'Tinashe stood on her tiptoes, stretching her neck to see...'**
    What does this suggest about Tinashe?

    | The labs didn't interest her. | She was eager to see the labs. | She was annoyed by her classmates. |

    Circle your answer.

    1 mark

Inference Questions

5) Read the paragraph beginning **'For as long as...'**

Find and copy a phrase which suggests that Tinashe owns lots of books about scientists.

....

....

1 mark

6) How can you tell that Tinashe already knew what a science lab looked like?

Give **one** way.

> Read the paragraph beginning
> 'Her eyes widened...' really carefully.

....

1 mark

7) **'"It's almost magical!"'**

Is this a fact or an opinion?

....

1 mark

8) Read the last two paragraphs of the text.

How can you tell that Tinashe didn't want to leave the science labs?

Give **one** way.

....

....

1 mark

Tellastauriuses can answer inference questions in their sleep. Tick to show how you got on with these pages.

Word Meaning Questions

Time to put those WORD MEANING skills to the test. Some words can be a little tricky, but you can often figure out what they mean by looking at what's around them in the text.

1) **'...trudged towards the towering brick buildings...'**

What does the word **'trudged'** tell you about how Tinashe was moving?

Tick **one** box.

She was running. ☐   She was skipping. ☐

She was walking confidently. ☐   She was walking slowly. ☐

1 mark

2) Find and copy a word that means 'really not looking forward to'.

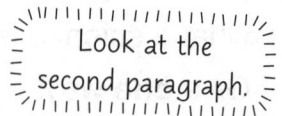

Look at the second paragraph.

....

1 mark

3) **'...books about famous inventors.'**

Circle the word which means the same as **'famous'** in this phrase.

| well-known | | strange | | forgotten | | clever |

1 mark

4) Draw a line to match each word to another word with a similar meaning.

peeked		shield
protect		fizzing
bubbling		glanced

1 mark

Tellastauriuses would rather work out word meanings than eat giant ice creams. How did you find this page?

The last few questions on Visiting Day are under here. ➡

2b # Fact Retrieval Questions

For these FACT RETRIEVAL questions, you'll need to look back through 'Crocodile Tale' to find the right information. See how you get on.

1) Who took Ella to the zoo?

....

_____
1 mark

2) Where was Ella when her mum told her to open her eyes? Circle your answer.

| in the shop | at the zoo entrance | in the Reptile Zone | in the car |

_____
1 mark

3) Write down **two** animals that Ella saw in the Reptile Zone.

....

....

_____
2 marks

4) Read the paragraph beginning **'Half of the enclosure was covered...'**
What colour was the crocodile's eye?

....

_____
1 mark

5) Why did Ella leave the Reptile Zone? Tick **one** box.

She was bored of looking at reptiles. ☐

Her mum wanted to get some lunch. ☐

It was closing for feeding time. ☐

There were too many people in the room. ☐

Think about what happened right before Ella and her mum left the Reptile Zone.

_____
1 mark

Section 3 — Crocodile Tale © *CGP — not to be photocopied*

Summary Question

2c

SUMMARY questions get you to think about more than just one part of the story — they might even be about the whole thing. Read the text again, then try this question.

1) Put these summaries of paragraphs in the order they happened in the story. The first one has been done for you.

The group set out on a tour of Caynton High. ☐

The science labs were described. ☐

Tinashe was excited when she first saw the labs. ☐

Tinashe worried about starting at Caynton High. **1**

_____
1 mark

Comparison Question

2h

COMPARISON questions ask you to take a look at things that are similar or different in the story. Give this question a go to put your comparison skills to the test.

1) a) By the end of the story, Tinashe felt differently about starting high school. How did her feelings change?

Tick **one** box.

She was more worried. ☐

She was less eager. ☐

She was less confused. ☐

She was more excited. ☐

_____
1 mark

b) Find and copy a phrase from the text to support your answer.

....

....
_____
1 mark

Tellastauriuses have won awards for their superb summary and comparison skills. How did you do?

At the very end of the room, a window stretched from wall to wall. It looked out onto a giant enclosure*.

Half of the enclosure was covered with long grass that sloped downhill into a big pond. Ella moved closer, searching for any signs of life. She jumped a little when she saw a single, yellow eye staring back at her from the water. A Nile* crocodile lay in shallow water at the edge of the pond, only a few metres from her. It was enormous — at least three times as long as Ella was tall.

She pressed her hands against the cool glass, studying the creature closely. She wished she could know what it felt like to be a crocodile, so strong and fierce. It must be amazing.

Then the reptile keeper called out. "Sorry folks, we're closing for feeding time. We'll reopen in an hour."

Ella sighed and reluctantly left the room, following her mum through the exit and into the gift shop.

"Mum, can I get a toy?" she asked.

"Go on then," her mum said, smiling. Ella immediately headed for a pile of fluffy toy crocodiles. She was about to pick one up when something else caught her eye. A beautiful, golden statue of a crocodile sat on a shelf above her head. Its eyes seemed to glitter playfully at her. She wasn't sure why, but she had a sudden urge to touch it. She slowly reached out her fingers. When she touched the statue, everything went black.

Glossary

enclosure — an area in a zoo where animals are kept
Nile — a river in north-eastern Africa

 ← *Keep turning...*

Crocodile Tale

"Where are we?" Ella asked, as her mum steered the car into a parking space.

"You'll find out soon enough," her mum said. "Keep your eyes closed. No peeking." Her mum guided her out of the car and she felt concrete beneath her feet. She could hear the chatter of groups of people growing louder as they walked, but she had no idea where they could be. A moment later, her mum stopped her. "Ready? Open your eyes."

"The zoo!" Ella said, staring up at the archway of the zoo entrance. A huge banner hung from it. It read:

"REPTILE ZONE NOW OPEN"

Ella squealed when she realised
why her mum had brought her there.
Ella loved reptiles, especially crocodiles
— they were her favourite animal. As soon as
her mum had bought the tickets, Ella grabbed
her hand and ran towards the Reptile Zone.

When they entered the dim room, Ella was amazed by the number of weird and wonderful creatures. They spent a long time wandering around reading facts about turtles, snakes and chameleons. Ella watched patiently as the animals steadily slithered around, moving cautiously through the leaves.

The story continues over the page.

Crocodile Tale

In this story, a girl called Ella goes on a trip to the zoo. She's excited
to see the crocodiles because they are her favourite animals.
However, she gets a bit closer to a crocodile than she expected...

What to do

1) Turn over the page, and read the story **Crocodile Tale**.

2) Then give the story another read through. This will help you
   make sure you haven't missed anything important.

3) Once you feel like you know the story well, have a go at the questions.

Ella blinked several times and a scene of sand, palm trees and a river came into view. She was lying on the bank of the River Nile.

She tried to speak, but no words came out. On either side of her, where her arms should have been, she saw huge, dark green legs and feet with sharp claws. She hurried to the edge of the bank and looked down at her reflection below. Two twinkling yellow eyes stared back at her.

"This is incredible," she thought. "I'm a crocodile!"

She slipped into the water and felt her powerful tail swishing behind her, driving her forwards. She shot up and down the river, rolling and diving under the cool water and enjoying the feeling of the warm sun on her back.

It seemed like she had been swimming for hours when she felt a hand on her shoulder. She looked round, but instead of seeing the river stretching out behind her, she saw her mum. She was back in the gift shop. Ella stared at the sparkling eyes of the crocodile statue in wonder.

"Have you picked something?" her mum asked.

"I'd like this, please," she said, lifting the statue carefully from the shelf.

"Are you sure you don't want a stuffed toy?" asked her mum, raising her eyebrows.

Ella grinned. "I'm really sure."

← *Open the flap for the start of the story.*

Section 3 — Crocodile Tale

Fact Retrieval Questions

2b

6) Put a tick in the correct box to show whether each statement is true or false.

	True	False
The crocodile at the zoo was in the water.		
Ella saw two crocodiles in the enclosure.		
The crocodile at the zoo was smaller than Ella.		

1 mark

7) Read the paragraph beginning **'"Go on then," her mum said, smiling...'**
Give **one** word in this paragraph that is used to describe the statue.

....

1 mark

8) Where did Ella go after she touched the statue?

a pond	the River Nile	a beach	a zoo

Circle your answer.

1 mark

9) Read the paragraph beginning **'She tried to speak...'**
Find and copy a phrase that tells you what Ella did at the edge of the bank.

....

1 mark

Tellastauriuses are pretty different from golden retrievers, but they're great at retrieving facts. How did you do?

Section 3 — Crocodile Tale

Inference Questions

Have a go at these INFERENCE questions. You'll need to think hard about what's really
happening in the story. Read through 'Crocodile Tale' again before you start.

1) Why did Ella's mum want Ella to keep her eyes closed at the start of the story?

....

1 mark

2) When Ella realised she was at the zoo, she felt

| nervous | annoyed | delighted | disappointed |

Circle your answer.

1 mark

3) Read the paragraph beginning **'When they entered the dim room...'**
What does this paragraph suggest about how the reptiles were moving?

Tick **one** box.

They were moving quickly. ☐

They were making a lot of noise as they moved. ☐

Think carefully about the words the writer has used.

They were moving slowly and carefully. ☐

They were leaping. ☐

1 mark

4) Ella was surprised when she first saw the crocodile at the zoo.
Find and copy the phrase that shows this.

Think about what Ella did when she saw the crocodile.

....

1 mark

2d

Inference Questions

5) Read from **'She pressed her hands...'** to **'...into the gift shop.'**
How can you tell that Ella was disappointed that she had to leave the Reptile Zone? Give **one** way.

....

1 mark

6) **'She tried to speak, but no words came out.'**
Why couldn't Ella speak?

Think about what had just happened to Ella at this point in the story.

....

1 mark

7) Read from **'She tried to speak...'** to **'...the warm sun on her back.'**
How do you think Ella felt about being a crocodile?
Explain your answer using evidence from the text.

....

....

2 marks

8) a) How did Ella's mum feel about Ella buying the crocodile statue?

| surprised | happy | angry | upset |

Circle your answer.

1 mark

b) How can you tell? Give **one** way.

Think about what Ella's mum did when Ella said she wanted the statue.

....

1 mark

---

*Tellastauriuses can't get enough of inference questions.
How did you find the questions on these pages?*

Word Meaning Questions

2a

WORD MEANING questions check that you understand certain words and phrases. If you don't know what something means, look at the rest of the sentence to help you work it out.

1) **'When they entered the dim room, Ella was amazed...'**
Circle the word which means the same as **'dim'** in this sentence.

small	cold	quiet	dark

_____
1 mark

2) **'Ella immediately headed for a pile of fluffy toy crocodiles.'**
Circle the word that means the same as **'immediately'** in this sentence.

slowly	uncertainly	instantly	excitedly

_____
1 mark

3) Read the paragraph beginning **'She tried to speak...'**
Find and copy a word that means 'rushed'.

....
_____
1 mark

4) **'Ella stared at the sparkling eyes of the crocodile statue in wonder.'**
Which of the words below is closest in meaning to the word **'sparkling'**?
Tick **one** box.

cold ☐   beautiful ☐

shining ☐   dull ☐

_____
1 mark

Tellastauriuses can pull meanings out of words like magicians can pull rabbits out of hats. How did you do?   ◯✓ ◯✓ ◯✓

The last few questions on <u>Crocodile Tale</u> are under here. ➡

"What?" she said, looking up suddenly. "Rudy? Where's Rudy? Isn't he with Freddie?"

I explained where he'd gone. Mum raced up to meet Freddie at the desk, dragging me behind her. Moments later, a member of staff was leading us all swiftly down the corridor. Mum's eyes searched frantically with each step. Freddie was calling Rudy's name every few seconds. Even though I knew he couldn't have gone far, I began to get a bit concerned when we got near the end of the corridor and still hadn't found him. Then, a flight attendant* appeared in the open door of the plane.

"Have you seen a small boy?" Mum asked, anxiously.
"Come this way," he replied, cheerfully.

The flight attendant led us to the cockpit*. There he was — the little troublemaker — sitting in the captain's chair, grinning like it was his birthday while the pilots explained to him what each of the buttons did.

Mum bolted forwards, scrambling to wrap Rudy up in an enormous hug. Me? I was relieved of course, but I couldn't stop thinking about how Rudy might actually fly planes one day. I shook my head in disbelief — what a terrifying thought...

Glossary

flight attendant — person who looks after passengers during a flight
cockpit — where the pilots of a plane sit

← *Open the flap for the start of the story.*

Ready for Take-Off

Sun, sea, and best of all, no school! Jetting off on a summer holiday sure is exciting. In 'Ready for Take-Off', there's plenty of excitement for Leo and his family before they've even left the airport...

What to do

1) Read the story **Ready for Take-Off**.

2) Then turn back to the start and read it one more time — this will help make sure you understand the tricky bits.

3) Once you've got to grips with the story, you're ready to start having a go at the questions.

Ready for Take-Off

My brother Rudy wants to fly when he's older. Planes or spaceships, it doesn't matter — if I'm honest, I'm not sure he knows the difference. I've seen more than one of his drawings where he's put a plane in space. To be fair, he's only five.

I'm eleven, but I wouldn't be a pilot or an astronaut for anything. Mum says that flying a plane is probably just like playing a video game, what with all the buttons and things, but I'm not so sure. I'd rather just earn money playing my video games. Rudy likes to watch me when I'm playing and I don't mind that. I teach him about different games and sometimes we even compete against each other. He's all right, is Rudy.

A couple of months ago, my mum's boyfriend, Freddie, announced that he was taking us all on holiday to Spain. Mum was grinning for days afterwards and spent ages planning activities for us to do while we were there. Freddie is also Rudy's dad. He's a fantastic cook — he makes the best burgers on the barbecue in summer. For the next two weeks we would be on holiday, so we were going to be enjoying those burgers in Spain.

I had only ever been out of the country once before, when my dad took me to New York five years ago. I don't really remember much of that trip, so I was really looking forward to having lots of new adventures abroad.

The story continues over the page.

Eventually, the day came for us to go to the airport — it was near London, so it was a bit of a trek. The four of us set off just as the sun began to rise, got to our gate* early and waited for our plane to start boarding*. While Freddie was at the desk asking about our seats on the plane, the pilots came past in their smart navy-blue uniforms, and headed down the corridor towards the plane, wheeling their suitcases behind them.

"Look, Rood," I said. "They're the pilots."

His eyes followed them as they walked.

"They're flying our plane?"
"That's right."

I looked for Mum to warn her that we must be about to board. She was deep in her handbag, digging through piles of junk because, somehow, she'd lost track of her passport* after she'd bought a cup of coffee. I turned back to Rudy — or, to where Rudy should have been... My eyes darted around. There he was, whizzing down the corridor after the pilots, arms out like an aeroplane. I sighed, preparing to break the news to Mum.

"Mum."
"Not now, dear."
"No, really. *Mum*."
"Leo, I've lost my passport. Can't it wait?"
"Mum, we've lost *Rudy*."

Glossary

gate — where you get on a plane
boarding — when people start getting on a plane
passport — a document which lets you travel to another country

← *Keep turning...*

Summary Questions

2c

SUMMARY questions ask you to think about bigger chunks of the text and describe what happens in just a few words. Read the story again, then try these summary questions.

1) Read from '**When they entered the dim room...**' to '**It must be amazing.**'
   Which of these sentences best summarises this section?

Ella entered the gift shop.	**Ella explored the Reptile Zone.**	**Ella read about turtles.**	**Ella and her mum left the zoo.**

Circle your answer.

_____
1 mark

2) The title of this text is '**Crocodile Tale**'.
   Suggest a different title you could use for this text.

Think about the main events in the text.

....

_____
1 mark

Prediction Question

2e

PREDICTION questions are all about working out what might happen next in the story. Have a go at this question about 'Crocodile Tale' to practise your prediction skills.

1) Which of the following is most likely to have happened when Ella took the crocodile statue home?

Tick **one** box.

She destroyed the statue.   ☐

She used the statue to become a crocodile again.   ☐

She gave the statue to her mum as a present.   ☐

_____
1 mark

Summary and prediction questions are no problem for a Tellastaurius. How did you find them?

© CGP — not to be photocopied

Section 3 — Crocodile Tale

2b Fact Retrieval Questions

For FACT RETRIEVAL questions, you need to hunt through the text and pick out bits of information. So, have a go at these questions and get searching.

1) According to the text, how old is Rudy?

....

1 mark

2) Give **two** jobs that Leo **doesn't** want to do in the future.

Read the second paragraph really carefully.

....

....

2 marks

3) Read the paragraph beginning **'A couple of months ago...'**
Who is Freddie? Tick **two** boxes.

Leo's dad ☐   Rudy's dad ☐

Leo's mum's boyfriend ☐   Leo's brother ☐

2 marks

4) How long were Leo and his family going on holiday for?

....

1 mark

5) Where did Leo go on his holiday five years ago?

Be careful — more than one of these places is mentioned in the story.

| Italy | London | Spain | New York |

Circle your answer.

1 mark

Fact Retrieval Questions

2b

6) Read the paragraph beginning **'Eventually, the day came...'**
Give **two** details about the pilots' uniforms.

Look for the words that have been used to describe the uniforms.

....

....

2 marks

7) Read the paragraph beginning **'I looked for Mum...'**
Why was Leo's mum looking through her handbag? Tick **one** box.

She was checking that she had everything. ☐

She had lost her mobile phone. ☐

She couldn't find her passport. ☐

She was taking rubbish out of her bag. ☐

1 mark

8) Read page 35.
Put a tick in the correct box to show whether each statement is true or false.
The first one has been done for you.

	True	False
Leo's mum looked for Rudy in the corridor.	✓	
Freddie didn't help to look for Rudy.		
The flight attendant knew where Rudy was.		

1 mark

9) Where was Rudy when his family found him?

....

1 mark

Tellastauriuses collect millions of facts and then display them in a museum. How did you get on?

Section 4 — Ready for Take-Off

Inference Questions

The next two pages are all about INFERENCE, which means you'll have to think about what the text means, not just what it says. Read the story again, then have a go at these questions.

1) Read the second paragraph.

   How can you tell that Leo and Rudy get on well? Give **one** way.

   ....
   _____
   1 mark

2) a) Read the paragraph beginning '**A couple of months ago...**'
   How did Leo's mum feel about going on holiday? Tick **one** box.

   > *Look at what Leo's mum did after she found out about the holiday.*

   shocked ☐   excited ☐

   annoyed ☐   nervous ☐
   _____
   1 mark

   b) Give **one** piece of evidence from the text to explain your answer.

   ....
   _____
   1 mark

3) Read the paragraph beginning '**Eventually, the day came...**'
   At what time of day did Leo and his family leave for the airport?

   | late in the evening | early morning | middle of the day | afternoon |

   Circle your answer.
   _____
   1 mark

4) '**His eyes followed them as they walked.**'
   What does this sentence suggest about what Rudy was doing?

   ....
   _____
   1 mark

2d # Inference Questions

5) Read the paragraph beginning **'I looked for Mum...'**
How do you think Leo feels about telling his mum that Rudy is missing?
Use evidence from the text to support your answer.

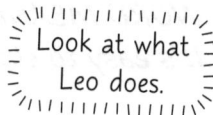

Look at what Leo does.

....

....

2 marks

6) Read the paragraph beginning **'I explained where...'**
Give **two** pieces of evidence that show Leo's mum and Freddie were panicking.

....

....

2 marks

7) Read the paragraph beginning **'The flight attendant led us to the cockpit...'**
Find and copy a phrase which tells you that Rudy was happy.

....

1 mark

8) Put a tick in the correct box to show whether each quotation is a fact
or an opinion. The first one has been done for you.

	Fact	Opinion
'I had only ever been out of the country once before'	✓	
'he makes the best burgers'		
'The flight attendant led us to the cockpit.'		

1 mark

Tellastauriuses aren't afraid of even the most mind-boggling inference questions. How did you do?

Word Meaning Questions

WORD MEANING questions get you thinking about what certain words in the text mean.
It's easy to slip up, so make sure you read each question carefully before you answer.

1) **'...sometimes we even compete against each other.'**
   What does the word **'compete'** mean in this sentence?

   Think about which word could replace 'compete' in this sentence.

play	defeat	help	attack

   Circle your answer.

   _____
   1 mark

2) Read the paragraph beginning **'Eventually, the day came...'**
   Find and copy a word which could be replaced with the phrase 'long journey'.

   ....

   _____
   1 mark

3) Read the paragraph beginning **'I looked for Mum...'**
   Which word in this paragraph tells you that Rudy was moving quickly?

   ....

   _____
   1 mark

4) **'I was relieved of course, but I couldn't stop thinking...'**
   Which of the words below is closest in meaning to **'relieved'** in this sentence?
   Tick **one** box.

hopeful	☐	shocked	☐
glad	☐	furious	☐

   _____
   1 mark

Tellastauriuses know even more word meanings than the dictionary. How did you find this page?

Summary Questions

2c

For *SUMMARY* questions, it's a good idea to read through the whole story again and really pay attention to what each section of the text is about. Give these questions a go.

1) Read from '**"What?"** she said, looking...' to '...open door of the plane.'
   Which sentence best summarises this section?

   Tick **one** box.

   Rudy's family are worried. ☐

   Leo's family are excited for their holiday. ☐

   Rudy is at the desk with Freddie. ☐

   Leo knows where Rudy is. ☐

   1 mark

2) The title of this text is **'Ready for Take-Off'**.
   Suggest a different title you could use for the text.

   ....

   1 mark

Language Question

2g

To answer *LANGUAGE* questions, you have to think about why a writer might have chosen to use the words and phrases that they have. Test your skills by trying out this question.

1) **'Mum bolted forwards, scrambling to wrap Rudy up in an enormous hug.'**
   Why do you think the writer chose the words **'bolted'** and **'scrambling'** to describe how Leo's mum was moving?

   ....

   ....

   1 mark

Tellastauriuses start every day with a nice selection of summary and language questions. How did you get on?

     Section 4 — Ready for Take-Off

Scoresheet

Great work, you're all finished with this book. Use the answer book to find out how well you did and write your marks in the table below.

		Section 1 – The Ghost	Section 2 – Visiting Day	Section 3 – Crocodile Tale	Section 4 – Ready for Take-Off	Total
2a	**Word Meanings**	/ 4	/ 4	/ 4	/ 4	/ 16
2b	**Fact Retrieval**	/ 9	/ 8	/ 10	/ 12	/ 39
2c	**Summarising**	/ 2	/ 1	/ 2	/ 2	/ 7
2d	**Inferences**	/ 8	/ 8	/ 10	/ 11	/ 37
2e	**Predictions**			/ 1		/ 1
2f	**Structure**	/ 1				/ 1
2g	**Language**				/ 1	/ 1
2h	**Comparisons**		/ 2			/ 2
	Total	/ 24	/ 23	/ 27	/ 30	/ 104

Look at your total score to see how you're doing and where you need more practice:

0 – 45 — Don't worry if you got lots wrong. Revise the reading skills you're struggling with and then have another go at the questions.

46 – 85 — You're doing well. Look back at any reading elements you're struggling with and try the questions again to make sure you're happy with them.

86 – 104 — Good work, you're doing great. Give yourself a pat on the back.

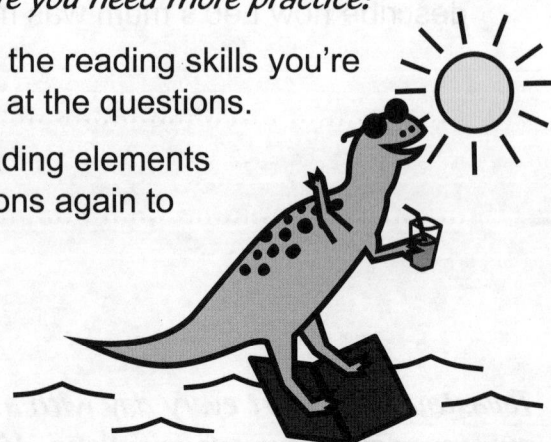